Killing Hogs and Curing Pork

by US Dept. of Agriculture

with an introduction by Sam Chambers

Self Reliance Books

Get more historic titles on animal and stock breeding, gardening and old fashioned skills by visiting us at:

http://selfreliancebooks.blogspot.com/

Introduction

I am pleased to present this reprinted edition of Us Department of Agriculture's famous book "Killing Hogs and Curing Pork". The book was first published in 1917 and contains important insights into the butchering and dressing of meat on the farm.

The work is in the Public Domain and is re-printed here in accordance with Federal Laws.

As with all reprinted books of this age that are intended to perfectly reproduce the original edition, considerable pains and effort had to be undertaken to correct fading and sometimes outright damage to existing proofs of this title. At times, this task is quite monumental, requiring an almost total "rebuilding" of some pages from digital proofs of multiple copies. Despite this, imperfections still sometimes exist in the final proof and may detract from the visual appearance of the text.

I hope you enjoy reading this book as much as I enjoyed re-publishing and making it available to fanciers again.

With Regards,

Sam Chambers

THE BUTCHER'S GUIDE

PORK.

1. Leg	4. Spare-rib
2. Hind-loin	5. Shoulder
3. Fore-loin	6. Brisket

LAMB.

1. Leg	5. Rack
2. Shoulder	6. Breast
3. Loin	7. Neck
4. Loin, chump-end	

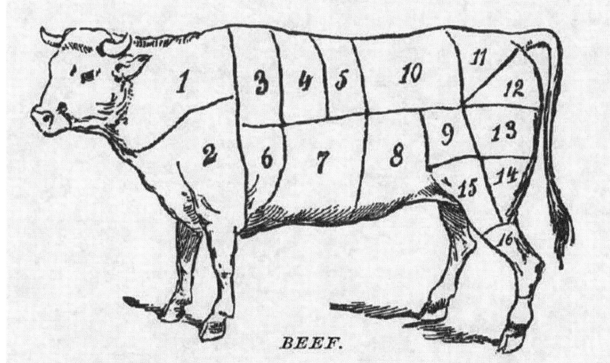

BEEF.

1. Neck	5. Fore-rib	9. Veiny piece	13. Round
2. Clod	6. Shoulder	10. Loin	14. Mouse-round
3. Chuck ribs	7. Brisket	11. Rump	15. Thick flank
4. Middle ribs	8. Thin flank	12. Aitch-bone	16. Shank

KILLING HOGS AND CURING PORK.

CONTENTS.

TOO MANY FARMERS buy a part or all of their supply of meat from local stores and hucksters. Meat, especially pork, can be grown and cured at home for much less than the cost of the purchased meat, to say nothing of a ready market for good country-cured hams, shoulders, and sides. In spite of this the custom of farmers purchasing cured meats is increasing. It may not be practicable for every farmer to butcher and cure his own meat, but in nearly every community a few farmers could do this and make good profits. Farmers who sell country-cured meats have experienced very little difficulty in establishing a permanent trade. To accomplish this one must understand the kind of cured meat his trade demands, and also how it is made. Country-cured meat often carries too much fat and undesirable odors, and it is generally too salty. A well marbled, juicy, savory piece of meat showing the proper admixture of fat and lean and possessing a good flavor is the kind the consumer desires.

SELECTION OF HOGS FOR BUTCHERING.

HEALTH.

In selecting hogs for butchering, health should have first consideration. Even though the hog has been properly fed and carries a prime finish, the best quality of meat can not be obtained if the animal is unhealthy; there is always some danger that disease may be transmitted to the person who eats the meat. The keeping quality of the meat is always impaired by fever or other derangements.

3

CONDITION.

A hog in medium condition, gaining rapidly in weight, yields the best quality of meat. Do not kill a hog that is losing flesh. A reasonable amount of fat gives juiciness and flavor to the meat, but large amounts of fat are not essential.

QUALITY.

The breeding of animals plays an important part in producing a carcass of high quality. Selection, long continued care and intelligent feeding will produce meat of desirable quality. The smooth, even, and deeply fleshed hogs will yield the nicely marbled meat.

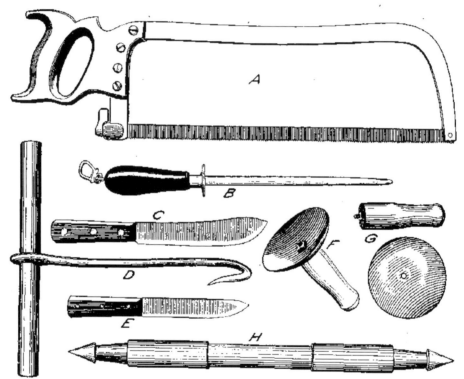

Fig. 1.—Tools for killing and dressing hogs.

AGE FOR KILLING.

The meat from very young hogs lacks flavor and is watery. Old meat is generally very tough. The meat of old hogs can be improved, however, if they are properly fattened before slaughter. Hogs can be killed for meat any time after 8 weeks, but the most profitable age at which to slaughter is 8 to 12 months.

CARE BEFORE KILLING.

Hogs intended for slaughter should remain unfed for at least 24 hours, or better, 30 hours. Give them all the clean, fresh water they will drink. This will help to clear the system of food and will facilitate bleeding. Do not excite or whip a hog before killing. An excited hog never makes a good carcass, and whipping causes bruised hams, which are not fit to cure. An injured hog may be used for food provided it is bled immediately.

EQUIPMENT FOR SLAUGHTERING.

It is essential to have the proper equipment for rapid and skillful work at killing time: An 8-inch straight sticking knife, a cutting

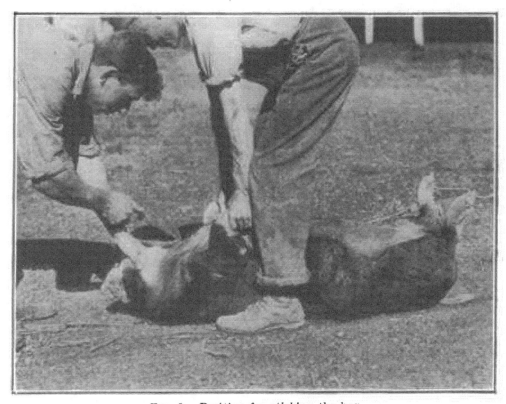

FIG. 2.—Position for sticking the hog.

knife, a 14-inch steel, a hog hook, a bell-shaped stick scraper, a gambrel, and a meat saw (fig. 1). More than one of each of these tools may be necessary if many hogs are to be slaughtered and handled to best advantage. A barrel is a very convenient receptacle in which to scald hogs. The barrel should be placed at an angle of about 45 degrees at the end of a table or platform of proper height. The table and barrel should be securely fastened to prevent accident to the workmen due to slipping. A block and tackle will reduce labor. All the tools and apparatus should be in readiness before beginning.

KILLING AND DRESSING.

Ordinarily it is not necessary to stun or shoot a hog before sticking, although this is done in some localities for humane reasons. If the hog is stuck without being stunned, he should be squarely on his back when stuck. Two men can reach under and grasp the legs on the opposite side of the body and with a quick jerk turn the hog over on his back. One man can stand astride the body with his legs just back of the hog's shoulders, taking a good grip on the forelegs (fig. 2). In this position the hog can be held in place while the other man does the sticking.

STICKING.

A narrow, straight-bladed knife, 8 inches long, serves very well for sticking a hog. The knife should be pointed directly toward

FIG. 3.—A convenient arrangement for scalding.

the root of the tail and held in a line with the backbone. Thrust the knife in 6 or 8 inches directly in front of the breastbone. The knife should be kept in a straight line so as not to stick a shoulder, causing blood to clot, which results in waste in trimming or a shoulder which keeps poorly. After the knife has been inserted 6 or 7 inches, turn it and withdraw. This severs the arteries in the neck and will insure better bleeding. Avoid sticking the heart, for if this is done the blood will not be pumped from the arteries. After sticking, the hog may be turned over on the side.

SCALDING AND SCRAPING.

The handiest way of heating water for scalding is in a large caldron or a kettle built for scalding hogs and which is placed over a fire near the place of butchering. A barrel is the most convenient receptacle in which to scald a hog, unless the hog is too large for the barrel, in which case a tank must be used. The best arrangement for most efficient scalding is shown in figure 3, and previously described in the paragraph entitled "Equipment for slaughtering." Much of the heavy labor can be avoided by means of a hoist, such as a block and tackle, for lifting the hog in and out of the scalding vat or when hanging the hog for removing the entrails.

If the water is heated in the house, it should be boiling when removed from the stove and carried to the barrel. At the time the hog is scalded the water should be at a temperature of 185° to 195° F. If no thermometer is at hand, stick the finger into the water three times in rapid succession, and if it burns severely the third time the water is about right. If the water is too hot the hair is likely to set, causing even more trouble than if too cold. A teaspoonful of lye or a small shovelful of wood ashes added to every 30 gallons of water will aid in removing the scurf. After either one of these alkalis is added the water should be stirred thoroughly.

Insert the hog hook in the lower jaw, place the hog on the table, and slide it into the barrel (fig. 3). The rear end of the hog is scalded first for the reason that if the water is too hot and the hair sets it can be removed easier from the rear than from the fore part of the hog. The hog should be kept moving in the water to be sure that no part will rest against the side of the barrel. Occasionally the hog should be drawn out of the water to air, when the hair may be "tried." When the hair and scurf slip easily from the surface, scalding is complete. Pull the hog out upon the table and remove the hair and scurf from the legs and feet at once. The simplest way to accomplish this is to twist the legs in both hands. Use the hog hook to remove the dewclaws at the same time. Remove the hair and scurf from the rear end of the hog by means of a bell-shaped scraper.

Cut the skin about 3 or 4 inches long just below the hocks in both hind legs. Loosen the tendons and insert the gambrel. Be sure that both tendons in each leg are loosened before inserting the gambrel. Now scald the front part of the hog. After the front part of the hog is scalded pull it out on the table as before. Remove the hair and scurf from the ears, forelegs, and head immediately, as these parts cool very quickly. Use the bell-shaped scraper to remove the remaining hair and scurf. If the hair fails to yield in any particular region, cover that portion with a gunny sack and pour on hot water.

When most of the hair and scurf is removed pour hot water over the entire carcass and shave off, by means of a knife, the hair that is left. Hang up the hog and pour a bucketful of cold water over the carcass and scrape from the surface the remaining dirt or scurf.

REMOVING ENTRAILS.

After the hog is hung up and the surface is clean the next step is to remove the entrails. Cut through the midline, beginning at the top and continue cutting down to the head. Cut around the rectum on each side and pull it out between the pelvic bones.

FIG. 4.—Removing the intestines.

Place the knife between the first and second fingers of the left hand, inserting the fingers where the opening has been made and with the right hand force the knife down to the breastbone (fig. 4). The fingers will serve as a guide in making the cut and protect the intestines from being cut. When this opening has been made remove the fat which surrounds the stomach. Then remove the intestines and stomach, cutting the gullet as soon as it is drawn up far enough. Cut on each side of the tongue to loosen it and pull it out with an upward jerk. Now cut through the breastbone, beginning at the front end. Cut upward slightly to one side. Remove the pluck, which consists of the heart, lungs, gullet, and windpipe, by cutting the diaphragm. This is the membrane which separates the organs of the chest from the stomach, bowels, and other abdominal organs. Cut just between the light and dark portions of the diaphragm.

Cut down along the backbone and it will be easy to pull out the entire pluck. Put a piece of corncob or small block of wood in the hog's mouth so air can circulate. Wash out the inside of the carcass with cold water and a cloth. Take a stick about a foot or 18 inches long and spread open the sides, allowing a free circulation of air. To facilitate cooling, the head can be removed and the carcass split or sawed down the backbone. In splitting or sawing the carcass be careful to cut as near the midline as possible.

THE LEAF LARD.

While the carcass is still warm, remove the leaf lard or kidney fat. This facilitates cooling the carcass and lessens the danger of the hams and loins souring. The leaf lard should be spread out on a table to cool, with the thin membrane side turned down. The gut fat should not be mixed with the leaf lard in rendering.

COOLING THE CARCASS.

The carcass should be cooled after slaughtering, but not allowed to freeze. Temperature can not be controlled on the farm, but it is possible to kill when the weather is favorable. Select a day in winter when there is chance for cooling the carcass before the surface freezes. The desirable temperature for cooling meat is 34 to 40° F. In the summer time it is necessary to have refrigeration. In the fall it is best to kill in the evening, allowing the carcass to cool overnight. Hang the carcass in a dark cellar or a cool room in the barn before the flies can get at it. Freshly killed meat absorbs odors very readily; do not hang the carcass in a freshly painted room or in a room with tar, kerosene, or gasoline.

A pork carcass should not be cut up until it is thoroughly cooled.

CUTTING UP HOGS.

The usual farm method of cutting up a hog is to sever the ribs on each side of the backbone, take out the backbone, and split the carcass down the mid-line. The ribs are taken out before the sides are "blocked." Another method is to split with a saw or cleaver as near the midline as possible. Then divide each half into four parts, head, shoulder, middle, and hams, as shown in figure 5, left side. Remove the leaf if this was not done before. Peel the leaf backward with the fingers, starting at the front end. The kidneys are in this fat.

HEAD.

The head is generally removed before the carcass is split into halves. Cut about an inch back of the ears, making a complete circle around the head. If the cut does not happen to strike the atlas joint,

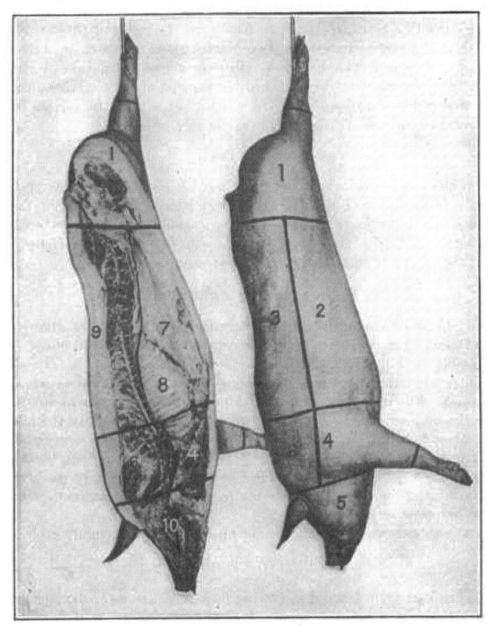

FIG. 5.—Cuts of pork: 1. Ham. 2. Bacon. 3. Loin. 4. Shoulder. 5. Head. 6. Plate. 7. Leaf lard. 8. Ribs. 9. Fat back.

twist the head and it will yield. The fattest part of the head can be used for lard and the more fleshy parts may be used for sausage or headcheese. The jowl is sometimes used for cooking with sauerkraut or baked beans and in the spring with turnip greens.

SHOULDER.

One-half the carcass should be placed on a cutting table and cut up into the various cuts shown in figure 5. Cut off the front foot about 1 inch above the knee and the hind foot the same distance above the hock. The feet can be used to make pickled pigs' feet or

FIG. 6.—The shoulder cuts and trimmings.

pigs' feet jelly. The shoulder cut is made between the fourth and fifth ribs. Remove the ribs from the shoulder, also the piece of backbone which may be attached. Cut close to the ribs in removing them so as to leave as much meat on the shoulder as possible.

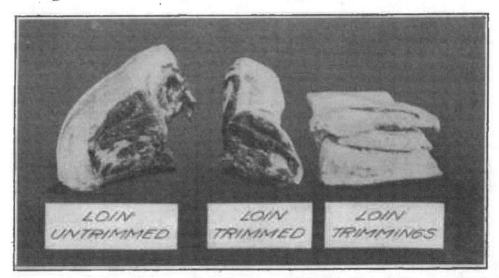

FIG. 7.—Loin, loin trimmings, and fat back.

These are "spare ribs" and make an excellent dish when fried or baked. If only a small amount of cured meat is desired, the top of the shoulder may be cut off about one-third the distance from the top and parallel to it (fig. 6). The fat of the shoulder top may be used for lard and the lean meat for steak or roasts. It should be trimmed up smoothly. The fat trimmings should be used for lard and the lean trimmings for sausage.

MIDDLE.

The ham is removed from the middle by cutting just back of the rise in the backbone. Cut from the flank toward the root of the tail to an angle of about 45°. Loin meat is thus saved which would otherwise be trimmed off the ham and used for sausage. Remove the ribs from the side, cutting as close to the ribs as possible. The loin and fatback are cut off in one piece; cut parallel with the back just below the tenderloin muscle on the rear part of the middle. Remove the fat on the top of the loin, but do not cut into the loin meat (fig. 7). The lean meat is used for chops or roasts and the fatback for lard. The remainder of the middle should then be trimmed for bacon. If it is a very large side it may be cut in two pieces. Trim all sides and edges as square as possible (fig. 9).

HAM.

All rough and hanging pieces of meat should be trimmed from the ham. The ham should then be trimmed smoothly, exposing as little lean meat as possible, because the curing hardens it (fig. 8). All lean trimmings should be saved for sausage and fat trimmings for lard. The other half of the carcass should be cut up in similar fashion.

MEAT TRIMMINGS AND FAT TRIMMINGS.

After the carcass has been cut up and the pieces are trimmed and shaped properly for the curing process, there are considerable pieces

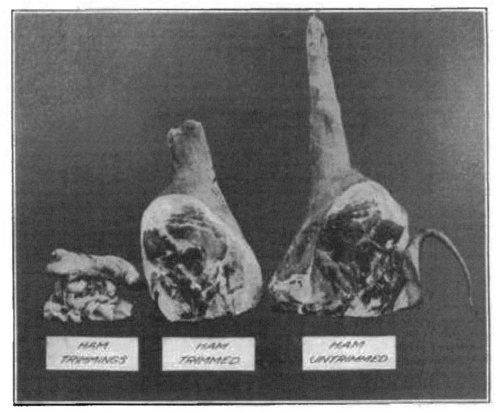

FIG. 8.—Ham and ham trimmings.

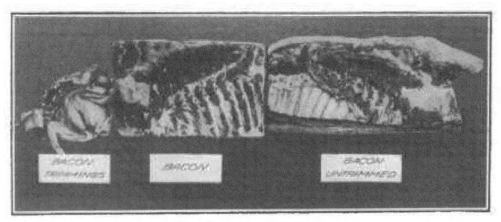

FIG. 9.—A side of bacon and bacon trimmings.

of lean meat, fat meat, and fat which can be used for making sausage and lard. The fat should be separated from the lean and used for lard. The meat should be cut into convenient pieces to pass through the grinder.

RENDERING LARD.

The leaf lard is of the best quality. The back strip of the side also makes good lard, as do the trimmings of the ham, shoulder, and neck. Intestinal or gut fat is an inferior grade and is best rendered by itself. It should be thoroughly washed and left in cold water for several hours before rendering, which will partially eliminate the offensive odor. Leaf lard, back strips, and lard trimmings can be rendered together. If the gut fat is included the lard takes on a very offensive odor.

First, remove all skin and lean meat from the lard trimmings. To do this cut the lard into strips about 1½ inches wide, then place the strip on the table, skin down, and cut the fat from the skin. When a piece of skin large enough to grasp is freed from the fat, take it in the left hand, knife held in the right hand inserted between the fat and skin, pull the skin and with the knife slanted downward slightly this

FIG. 10.—Pieces of fat cut for rendering.

will cleanly remove the fat from the skin. The strips of fat should then be cut into pieces of 1 to 1½ inches square, making them about equal in size so they try out evenly (fig. 10).

Pour into the kettle about a quart of water, then fill it nearly full with the lard cuttings. The fat will then heat and bring out the grease without burning. Cook the lard over a moderate fire. When starting the temperature should be about 160° F. and should be run up to 195° F. Frequent stirring is necessary to prevent burning (fig. 11). When the cracklings are brown in color and light enough to float, the lard should be removed from the fire. Press the fat from the cracklings and use them to make crackling bread or feed them to the chickens. When the lard is removed from the fire, allow it to cool a little. To aid cooling stir the lard. This also tends to whiten the lard and make it smooth. Then strain it through a muslin cloth into the containers.

When removing lard from a container for use, take it off evenly from the surface exposed. Do not dig down into the lard and take out a scoopful for when this is done it will leave a thin coating around the sides of the container which will become rancid very quickly by the action of the air.

CURING PORK.

The first essential in curing is to make sure the pork is thoroughly cooled. Meat should never be frozen either prior to or during the period of curing.

The proper time to begin curing is when the meat is cooled and still fresh. Twenty-four to 36 hours after killing is the opportune time.

VESSELS FOR CURING.

A clean hardwood molasses or sirup barrel is a suitable vessel in which to cure pork. The barrel should be clean and tight so as to prevent leakage. A large stone or metal jar is the best container in which to cure meat, but the initial cost is high. Stone or metal containers are very easily kept clean. If a barrel is used repeatedly for curing pork it is necessary to scald it out thoroughly before fresh pork is packed into it.

CURING AGENTS.

Salt, saltpeter, sugar, and molasses are the principal preservatives used in curing pork. Borax, boric acid, formalin, salicylic acid, and other chemicals are sometimes used, but their use is prohibited in connection with meats and products to which the Federal meat-inspection law is applicable.

Salt when applied alone to meat makes it very hard and dry, because its action draws out the meat juices and hardens the muscle fibers. Saltpeter is used to preserve the natural color of the meat.

It is more astringent than salt and should be used sparingly. Sugar and molasses act differently than salt. They soften the muscle fibers and improve the flavor of the meat, hence the combination of salt and sugar make a good cure.

BRINE CURING AND DRY CURING.

Much diversity of opinion exists as to the merits of the two ways of curing—brining and dry curing. It is less trouble to pack meat in a barrel and pour on brine than to rub meat three or four times with salt. The brine keeps away insects and vermin. If directions are followed closely and pure water is used in making the brine, it will not spoil and should keep for a reasonable length of time. If

Fig. 11.—A suitable kettle for rendering lard.

the brine becomes "ropy," it should be poured off and boiled or a new brine made. A cool cellar is the most desirable place for both brine and dry curing, though more moisture is required for dry curing. When meat is cured during warm weather the dry salt method of curing is far safer than the brine method.

It is advisable to rub with fine salt the surface of the meat and allow it to drain, flesh side down, for 6 to 12 hours before being put in the cure. This applies to both brine and dry curing.

BRINE-CURED PORK.

There are many different formulas for curing pork by the brine method, but the recipe given below if followed closely will give very good results.

For each 100 pounds of meat use—

    8 pounds salt.
    2½ pounds sugar or sirup.
    2 ounces saltpeter.
    4 gallons of water.

In warm weather 9 or 10 pounds of salt are preferable.

Allow four days' cure for each pound in a ham or shoulder and three days for bacon and small pieces. For example, a 15-pound ham will take 60 days; a piece of bacon weighing 10 pounds, 30 days.

The brine should be made the day before it is used, so that it will be cool. All the ingredients are poured into the water and boiled until thoroughly mixed. Place ham on the bottom of the container, shoulders next, bacon sides and smaller cuts on top. Pour in the brine, and be sure it covers the meat thoroughly. In five days pour off the brine and change the meat, placing the top meat on the bottom and the bottom meat on top, then pour back the brine. Repeat this operation again on the tenth and eighteenth days. If the pickle becomes ropy, take out all the meat and wash it off thoroughly, also the container. Boil the ropy pickle; or, better, make new pickle. When each piece of meat has received the proper cure, take it out of the pickle and wash in lukewarm water, string, and hang in the smokehouse. (See page 26 for directions for smoking.) The temperature of the smokehouse should not exceed 125° F. Smoke the meat until it has a good chestnut color.

An excellent cure, in which the meat is preserved in brine formed from the mixture of the juices brought out of the meat by the application of the following ingredients:

For each 100 pounds of meat use—

    8½ pounds salt.
    2 pounds melted sugar or warm sirup.
    2 ounces saltpeter.
    2 ounces red pepper.
    2 ounces black pepper.

All the ingredients should be mixed thoroughly. Rub each piece of meat with the mixture. Pack the meat in a container, hams on the bottom, shoulders next, and bacon sides on top. Enough liquid will be formed to cover the hams. Allow the meat to cure for six weeks; string and hang in the smokehouse. (See page 26 for directions for smoking.) The bacon and smaller pieces of meat, after they are cured, should be eaten first. The hams are better after they have aged.

DRY-CURED PORK.

Dry-cured pork requires more work than brine-cured, though it is sometimes less expensive. Danger from rats and other vermin is less in the case of brine-cured pork. Both methods of curing are very successful if care is taken to see that each operation is executed correctly. Following is the method of dry curing:

For each 100 pounds of meat use—
  7 pounds salt.
  2¼ pounds sugar.
  2 ounces saltpeter.

Mix all ingredients thoroughly, then rub one-third of the quantity of this mixture over the meat and pack it away in a box or on a table. The third day break bulk and rub on half of the remaining mixture over the meat and again pack the meat. Break bulk the seventh day and rub the remainder of the mixture over the meat and pack the meat to cure. Allow one day and a half cure for each pound the pieces of meat average. After the meat has cured, wash each piece with lukewarm water and hang in the smokehouse. (See page 26 for directions for smoking.)

Another dry cure is as follows:

For each 100 pounds of meat use—
  8 pounds salt.
  3 pounds warm syrup.
  2 ounces saltpeter.
  3 ounces black pepper.
  2 ounces red pepper.

All the above ingredients should be mixed together thoroughly. Rub each piece of meat thoroughly with this mixture and pack the meat in bulk on a clean floor or table or in a container. In 10 days break bulk and repack the meat. This is done to make the cure more uniform and to prevent souring. Allow the meat to cure five or six weeks. (See page 26 for directions for smoking.)

PICKLED PORK.

Fat backs cut into suitable pieces for curing are generally treated in the following manner: The pieces of meat are packed in a con-

tainer and a pickle made of the following ingredients is poured over
the meat: To 4 gallons of water add 10 pounds of salt and 2 ounces
of saltpeter for each 100 pounds of meat.

THE SMITHFIELD HAM.

Smithfield hams are cured as follows:

The hams are placed in a large tray of fine Liverpool salt, then
the flesh surface is sprinkled with finely ground crude saltpeter until
the hams are as white as though covered by a moderate frost—or,
say, use 3 to 4 pounds of the powdered saltpeter to the thousand
pounds of green hams.

After applying the saltpeter, salt immediately with the Liverpool
fine salt, covering well the entire surface. Now pack the hams in
bulk, but not in piles more than 3 feet high. In ordinary weather
the hams should remain thus for three days.

Then break bulk and resalt with the fine salt. The hams thus
salted and resalted should now remain in salt in bulk one day for
each and every pound each ham weighs—that is, a 10-pound ham
should remain 10 days, and in like proportion of time for larger and
smaller sizes.

Next wash with tepid water until the hams are thoroughly cleaned,
and, after partially drying, rub the entire surface with finely ground
black pepper.

Now the hams should be hung in the smokehouse and the important operation of smoking begun. The smoking should be done
very gradually and slowly, lasting 30 to 40 days.

After the hams are cured and smoked they should be repeppered,
to guard against vermin, and then bagged. These hams improve
with age and are in perfection when 1 year old.

SAUSAGE.

If made into sausage, scraps and pieces of meat which otherwise
would be wasted may be converted into delicious dishes. Sausage
making is a trade well worth learning. Often on the farm when
animals are butchered for home consumption portions of the carcass
are not utilized to best advantage. A demand for fresh and smoked
country sausage always exists, and it is just as important for every
farmer to know how to make good sausage as it is to know how to
make good hams and bacon.

The only equipment necessary to make sausage is a meat cutter
with a stuffer attachment. A very convenient grinder can be purchased for $3, and stuffer attachment will cost about 35 cents. A

knife, cord string, and casings or muslin bags also will be needed. The muslin bags can be made any size, but the most convenient are 12 inches long by 2 inches in diameter. When sausage is stuffed in muslin bags it should be paraffined after stuffing. Sausage stuffed in muslin bags and paraffined keeps longer and better than sausage in casings. Sausage will keep very well in stone crocks or tin pans if a layer of lard or paraffin is put over the top.

PURE PORK SAUSAGE.

Good pork sausage may be made as follows: Take three parts of fresh lean meat to one part of fat. Add to each 100 pounds of meat $1\frac{1}{2}$ to 2 pounds salt, 2 ounces fine sage, 1 ounce ground nutmeg, and 4 ounces black pepper. Cut the meat into small pieces and then put through the grinder, using the small plate. The spices should all be mixed together and added to the meat as it goes through

FIG. 12.—A display of various kinds of sausage.

the grinder. After it is well ground, mix thoroughly, to be sure that it is uniformly flavored. No water should be added if the sausage is stored away in bulk. If stuffed in casings, a little water is necessary to soften the meat so that it will slip through the stuffer into the casings.

SMOKED SAUSAGE OR COUNTRY SAUSAGE.

The following ingredients are used in making smoked or country sausage:

        85 pounds lean pork.
        15 pounds beef.
        1½ to 2 pounds salt.
        4 ounces black pepper.
        1 ounce red pepper.
        1 ounce sweet marjoram.
        1 ounce mace.

Cut the meat into small pieces and sprinkle seasoning over it, then run through the grinder with the small plate. Put it away in a cool place for 24 to 36 hours, then add a little water, and stuff into hog casings and smoke in a very cool smoke until a dark mahogany color is obtained.

FRANKFORT OR VIENNA STYLE SAUSAGE.

Frankfort or Vienna style sausage is more popular with the manufacturers and the trade than any other kind of sausage. It is made as follows:

        70 pounds beef.
        30 pounds pork (not too lean).
        20 pounds water.
        1½ to 2 pounds salt.
        2 ounces nutmeg.
        ¼ ounce black pepper.
        1 to 2 ounces red pepper.

Cut the beef into small pieces and salt and allow it to cure for 48 hours in a cool place. Cut the pork into small pieces and put the beef and pork through the grinder together. Put into a container and add the water and spices. After it is all mixed, put it through the grinder again, using the fine plate. Stuff into sheep casings. After the sausage is stuffed into the casings by means of the thumb and forefinger, press the casing together, about 4 inches apart. Twist the first link two or three times. The next link made should be twisted in the opposite direction to keep the casing from untwisting. After it is twisted into links, hang it in the smokehouse for about 2 hours at a temperature not to exceed 125° F. After it is smoked, boil it for 5 or 10 minutes and then plunge it into cold water and hang it in a cool place.

BOLOGNA STYLE SAUSAGE.

Bologna style sausage is used extensively for lunches on picnics or outings. Its keeping qualities are excellent. The following ingredients are used in making it:

60 pounds cured beef.[1]
40 pounds pork.
20 pounds water.
1½ to 2 pounds salt.
2 ounces mace.
1 ounce coriander.
4 ounces black pepper.

Grind the beef and let it cure for 24 to 36 hours in a cool place, then grind it very fine. Put the pork through the grinder, using the medium plate only once. Then put the beef and pork together in a container and add the spices and water. Mix thoroughly until it takes on a dull color and becomes sticky. Stuff in wesands, large beef casings, or in beef rounds. Allow it to hang about 20 minutes in a cool place. This sausage can also be stuffed into muslin bags and paraffined. It will keep perfectly prepared in this way. Smoke for about 2 hours, or until a good color is obtained, at a temperature not to exceed 140° F. After the bologna is smoked it should be boiled, the wesands and rounds about 30 minutes and the larger bolognas about 1½ hours, at a temperature of 160° F. To tell when bologna is cooked enough, squeeze it in the hand, and if done it will squeak when the pressure is released. Place in cold water for about 30 minutes and then hang it up in a cool place to keep.

BLOOD SAUSAGE.

Blood sausage is made of the following ingredients:

25 pounds cured back or shoulder fat.
7 pounds cured fat skins.
6 pounds blood.
½ pound onions.
1 pound salt.
½ ounce white pepper.
1 ounce sweet marjoram.
½ ounce cloves.

Cook the fat for about 1 hour and the skins 2 hours at a temperature of 200° F. When cooked put through grinder, using small or medium plate. Put into a container, add blood and seasoning, and mix thoroughly. Stuff into large beef casings and boil in the same water that the meat was cooked in until the sausage floats. Then dip the sausages into cold water and hang away to cool.

HEADCHEESE.

The head is generally used for making headcheese, but odds and ends also can be used. The head should be shaved clean, the snout

---

[1] Beef, ground, salt and seasoning added, and the bulk stored away for 36 to 48 hours before using it for sausage. Fresh meat stuffed into casings and smoked invariably spoils.

skinned and nostrils cut off just in front of the eyes. Cut out the eyes and the ear drums. The fattest part of the head is generally used for lard. When the head is cleaned, soak it in water for some time to extract the blood and dirt. After the head is thoroughly cleaned cover it with water and boil until the meat separates from the bones. Tongues and hearts may be cooked with the head. When this is thoroughly cooked take out the meat, saving the liquor for future use. Chop the meat up finely. Season with $1\frac{1}{2}$ pounds salt, 3 ounces black pepper, 4 ounces allspice, and 4 ounces ground cloves, together with 2 gallons of the liquor for every 50 pounds of meat. This should all be mixed thoroughly so that proper seasoning is secured. If casings can be obtained, stuff the mixture into large beef casings. A hog stomach, after it is thoroughly cleaned, can be used. If the meat is stuffed into casings, it should be boiled again in the same liquor in which the meat was previously boiled. The meat in the casings should be boiled until it floats on the top, then placed in cold water for a short time. Store it away in a clean, cool place on a shelf or table. Place a board over the meat in the casings with a weight on top in order to hold the shape and to prevent the moisture from collecting in one spot. If there are no casings available in which to stuff the meat, it can be kept in shallow pans.

LIVER SAUSAGE OR PUDDING.

All the odds and ends resulting from cutting up the hog carcass can be used in making liver sausage. The head, if used, should be cleaned as previously described under "Headcheese." The jowl may be cut off and salted down. The head, liver cut into slices, and some beef or veal, if any is at hand, should all be put into a kettle and boiled. The skin cut from the fat can also be boiled with this meat. The skin will be cooked before the meat, so it should be put into a cloth sack and removed when thoroughly cooked. Livers also cook in a very short time, and should be removed. The meat should cook until it falls from the bones. All the meat should be ground, using the small grinder plate. Add $1\frac{1}{2}$ pounds salt, 3 ounces sweet marjoram, 1 ounce allspice, 1 ounce black pepper, and about 1 gallon soup (the broth the meat was cooked in). Garlic or onions can be added if desired. This recipe is for every 40 pounds of meat. The seasoning should be worked into the meat. This finished product can be put into jars covered with paraffin or stuffed into beef rounds. When stuffed into casings, it should be cooked in the same water the meat was cooked in until the sausage floats. Then place in cold water until the sausage is thoroughly cooled.

SUMMER SAUSAGE.

The following ingredients are used to make summer sausage:

25 pounds cured beef free from sinews.
15 pounds pork trimmings.
6 ounces white pepper.
1 ounce whole black pepper.
1 ounce whole mustard seed.

This sausage can only be made in cold weather. All the meat is put through the grinder and spices added. No salt is needed, the cured beef being salty enough. Mix it all thoroughly until it is evenly seasoned. Spread it out in a cool place and leave it for 36 to 40 hours. Then stuff it into hog bung casings and let hang overnight. Smoke over very cool smoke for several days. This sausage can be kept in a dry place the year round. If it gets moldy, simply wipe off the mold before using it.

SCRAPPLE.

The head and feet of hogs are generally used in making scrapple, but scrapple can be made from any hog meat. The heads should be split through the middle and placed in a kettle with sufficient water to cover them. They should be cooked until the meat falls from the bones. Drain off the broth. Pick all the bones out of the meat, then chop the meat finely, add it to the broth and boil. Corn meal should be slowly added until it is as thick as mush. Add the corn meal slowly and stir vigorously, so as to avoid lumpiness. Stir the mixture well for 10 or 15 minutes and allow it to boil one hour, when it should be thick like mush. Pour the scrapple into shallow pans or molds. When cold, it can be sliced and fried.

SMOKING CURED MEAT.

The process of smoking helps to preserve the meat. Smoking also gives a desirable flavor to the meat, if it is smoked properly and with the right kind of fuel.

THE SMOKEHOUSE.

The smokehouse can be made any size and of the kind of material suitable to the demands of the owner. If a very small quantity of meat is to be smoked once a year, a barrel or a box (fig. 13) will answer. On the other hand, if a considerable quantity of meat is smoked and the house is to be permanent, it should be built of brick, concrete, or stone to be fireproof (figs. 14, 15.) A small outdwelling can be used if care is taken to confine the fire to the center of the room in an iron kettle. The safest method is to construct a fire pit

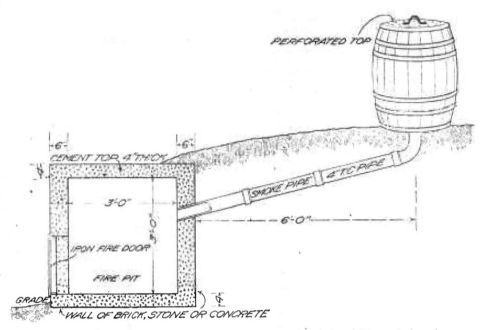

FIG. 13.—A type of smokehouse that can be constructed quickly and cheaply.

FIG. 14.—A farm smokehouse, fireproof and fairly tight.

outside of the house and pipe the smoke into the house. The pipe running from the pit to the house should be buried to prevent crushing.

. A smokehouse 6 by 8 feet, 10 feet high, will give best results for general farm use. Ventilation should be provided to carry off the

FIG. 15.—Meat curing and smoking house. (Built in Georgia after plans by United States Department of Agriculture.)

warm air and prevent overheating of the meat. Small openings under the eaves or a chimney in the roof will control ventilation. If arrangements can not be made to have a fire pit outside the house, it can be built on the floor and a metal sheet constructed to shield the meat. If the meat can be hung 6 or 7 feet above the fire, this shield will not be necessary. At this height the meat will get the benefit of the thick smoke and still hang below the ventilator.

THE FUEL.

Green hickory or maple wood is the best fuel for smoking. Hard wood is preferable to soft wood. Resinous woods should never be used, as they give an objectionable flavor to the meat. Corn cobs may be used, but they deposit carbon on the meat, giving it a dirty appearance.

SMOKING.

Meat should be removed from the brine when it is cured and not allowed to remain in the brine over time. When the meat is removed from the brine it should be soaked for about half an hour in water.

FIG. 16.—Meat hanging in the smokehouse.

If meat has remained in the brine longer than the allotted time, soak each piece half an hour and 3 minutes extra for each day over time. The meat should then be washed in lukewarm water, strung, and hung in the smokehouse. Do not hang the meat so that the pieces touch. (Fig. 16.) The space between the meat is necessary to insure good circulation of smoke around the meat. Permit the meat to hang in the smokehouse for 24 hours before beginning to smoke. A slow fire should be started, so that the meat will warm up gradually. Do not get the house too hot. The fire can be kept going continuous until the smoking is complete, holding the temperature as even as possible (120° F.). Thirty-six to 48 hours is the time required to smoke a lot of meat, but if the meat is intended to be kept for any length of time slower and longer smoking is desirable. During warm weather it is better to start the fire every other day rather than heat up the meat too much. In the winter, however, if the fire is not kept going the meat may cool and the smoke will not penetrate properly. As soon as the meat is thoroughly smoked, open the doors and ventilator, so that the meat can cool. When the meat is smoked it can hang in the smokehouse, but for absolute safe-keeping it should be wrapped or packed away.

PRESERVING SMOKED MEATS.

Smoked meat after it is hard and firm should be wrapped in heavy paper and put into muslin sacks. It is very important that the top of the sack be tied properly so as to keep out insects. Cut the strings from the hams or bacons before they are placed in the sacks. There is a great tendency to use the same string to hang up the meat after it is sacked. It is impossible to tie the top of the sack and make it insect proof if a string sticks out of the top. In tying the top of the sack make a double wrap before tying a knot and this will prevent the entrance of any insects. Each sack should be painted with yellow wash and then each piece can be hung up for future use. Never stack the hams and bacons in a pile after yellow wash has been applied.

RECIPE FOR YELLOW WASH.

For 100 pounds hams or bacons use—
  3 pounds barium sulphate.
  0. 06 pound glue.
  0. 08 pound chrome yellow.
  0. 40 pound flour.

Half fill a pail with water and mix in the flour, dissolving all lumps thoroughly. Dissolve the chrome yellow in a quart of water in a separate vessel and add the solution and the glue to the flour; bring the whole to a boil and add the barium sulphate slowly, stirring constantly. Make the wash the day before it is required. Stir it frequently when using, and apply with a brush.

SHIPPER'S CERTIFICATE.

Farmers who ship their cured meats must comply with official State and Federal regulations. Below appears a sample shipper's certificate such as must be used in interstate shipments of uninspected meat or meat food products which are from animals slaughtered by the farmer on the farm. In providing blank certificates for this purpose this sample should be followed. In size it should be 5½ by 8 inches.

SHIPPER'S CERTIFICATE.

Date_____, 191

Name of carrier_____

Shipper_____

Point of shipment_____

Consignee_____

Destination_____

I hereby certify that the following-described uninspected meat or meat food products are from animals slaughtered by a farmer on the farm, and are offered for transportation in interstate or foreign commerce as exempted from inspection according to the act of Congress of June 30, 1906, and at this date they are sound, healthful, wholesome, and fit for human food, and contain no preservative or coloring matter or other substance prohibited by the regulations of the Secretary of Agriculture governing meat inspection.

Kind of product.	Amount.	Weight.

Two copies of this form to be presented to the common carrier with each shipment.

....
(Signature of shipper.)

....
(Address of shipper.)

ECONOMIC SUGGESTIONS.

Cleanliness is the most important factor in butchering and curing meats. Meat very easily becomes tainted.

Save all pieces of meat for sausage. There are many ways of converting it into a palatable product.

All waste fat, trimmings, and skin should be rendered and the product used to make soap.

Bones should be crushed or ground for chicken feed.

Never put meat in cure before the animal heat is out of it.

Always pack meat skin side down when in the curing process; except the top layer in a brine cure, which should be turned flesh side down.

Keep close watch on the brine; and if it becomes "ropy," change it.

Do not forget to turn or change meat several times during the curing process.

The fat of dry-cured meat will sometimes become yellow. This does not make it unwholesome.

It takes more time to smoke dry-cured than brine-cured pork.

Slow smoking is much better than a rapid smoking, and there is less chance of causing the meat to drip.

If meat becomes moldy, brush off the mold with a stiff brush or trim off the moldy parts with a knife. The entire piece is not spoiled.

Be sure meat is thoroughly cooled before sacking.

Remember, the seasoning of sausage is generally governed by taste.

Fresh sausage can be kept under a covering of lard for a number of days.

KEEPING FRESH MEAT.

Fresh meat is difficult to keep during the summer months without the use of ice. Even with ice very little can be handled at one time on the average farm. If a room or family refrigerator can be kept at a temperature of 40° or less, with a good circulation of air, fresh meat can be kept for a week or 10 days. The air should be dry, because moisture in a refrigerator tends to develop wet mold or slime, which will spoil the entire piece of meat. If there is an ice house on the farm, a small portion of it may be partitioned off as a cold-storage room. The ice can then be properly packed on three sides of it, and with good drainage this makes a very satisfactory place for keeping meat. This space may also be used for storing butter, poultry, or other perishable products.

A SMALL ICE HOUSE.

To keep perishable products for a considerable time, some farmers may find it convenient and necessary to build a small ice house, which is not unduly expensive and has the advantages of saving perishable products that otherwise would spoil. The following description, plans, and bill of necessary materials [1] will assist in the construction of a small ice house.

METHOD OF BUILDING THE HOUSE.

Cut four pieces of rough 2 by 6 inch scantling 4 feet $10\frac{1}{2}$ inches long and spike them together in pairs to make the girders. (See A,

---

[1] Prepared by G. H. Parks, Meat Inspection Division of the Bureau of Animal Industry.

figs. 18, 19, 20, 21, 22.) Cut four pieces of rough 2 by 6 inch scantling 6 feet 5 inches long and set them on edge, spaced as shown in figure 19, on the girders which are to be placed at the extreme ends of the joist. The frame should now be turned over and the first layer of floor boards (marked C, figs. 18, 19, and 21) nailed to the joists. The floor boards should be cut so that they will just come to the outside edge of the joists (see C, figs. 19 and 21).

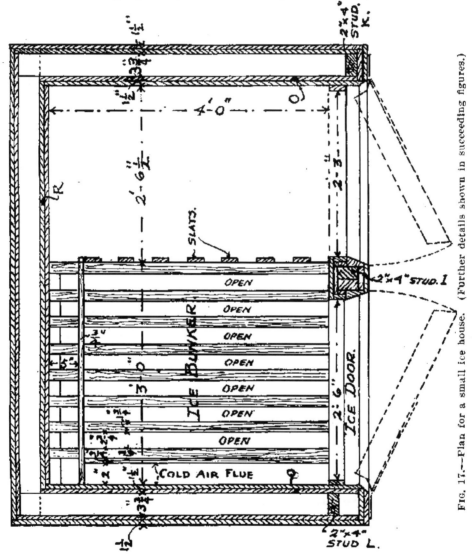

FIG. 17.—Plan for a small ice house. (Further details shown in succeeding figures.)

Over the flooring put on a layer of building paper. Cut the paper long enough to be turned up at least 4 inches on the outside face of the joists. The next layer of boards is now put on over the paper. The boards should be cut long enough to extend the thickness of the board beyond the outside face of the joists (see D, figs. 18, 19, and 21).

In figuring the drawings it is assumed that the 2 by 4's are dressed four sides, that they will measure 1¾ by 3¾ inches, and that the flooring is three-fourths inch thick.

The platform is now ready to be turned over and the ends of the girders nailed on posts which are buried in the ground about 2 feet and extend above the ground about 10 inches, so that a bucket can be placed under the drain pipe to catch the water from the melting ice and to form a trap (figs. 18 and 22).

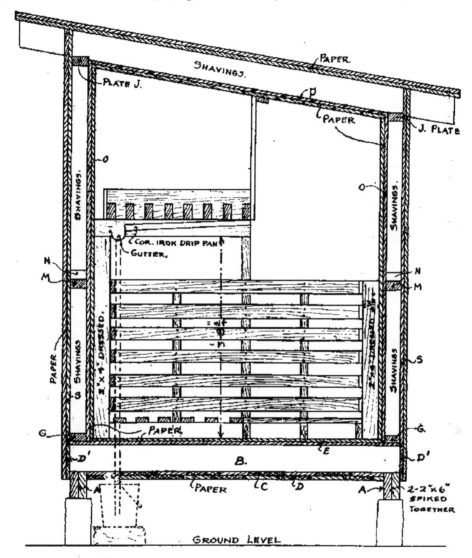

FIG. 18.—Longitudinal section of ice house.

Cut two pieces of boards 8 inches wide and 4 feet 10½ inches long and nail across the ends of the joist, placing the top edge of the board flush with the tops of the joists (see D, figs. 18 and 19). Fill the spaces formed by the joists and the end boards with dry mill shavings, using about 100 pounds.

A layer of matched and dressed boards (marked E, figs. 18, 19, 21, and 22) should now be nailed on the joists. The floor should begin

and end flush with the ends of the joists and not extend over the
boards nailed to the ends of the joists (see E, figs. 18 and 21). On
the long side of the platform nail a 2 by 4 laid flatwise the full length
of the platform (see F, figs. 19 and 22). Across one end nail flatwise a 2 by 4 cut 4 feet 3 inches long and on the other end nail a

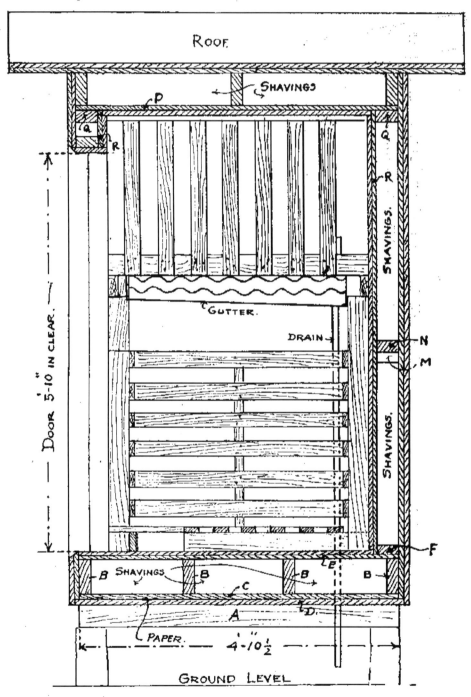

FIG. 19.—Cross section of ice house.

2 by 4 cut 4 feet 6¾ inches long, both 2 by 4's to start from the ends
of the 2 by 4 marked F in figures 19 and 22. (See G, figs. 18 and 21.)

Erect a 2 by 4 stud at the end of each 2 by 4 marked G, setting
the studs so that the width of the stud will be parallel with the long
side of the platform. The face of stud K will be flush with the

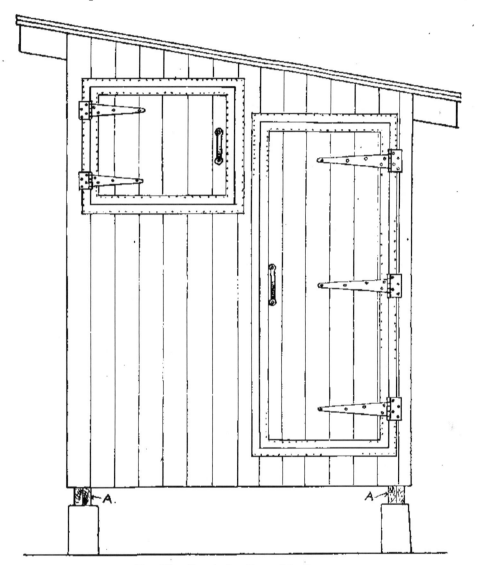

FIG. 20.—Front elevation of ice house.

outside edge of the platform, and the outside edge of stud L will be
3¾ inches back from the same face. (See figs. 17, 21, and 22.)

Cut two pieces of 2 by 4 inch 4 feet 10½ inches long for plates
(plates marked J, figs. 18, 21, and 22). Cut the corner stud marked
K, in figures 17 and 21, 5 feet 11 inches long and the stud marked L,
in figures 17 and 21, 6 feet 11 inches long.

Now cut a 2 by 4 inch 3 feet 7½ inches long (marked H, fig. 21) and nail it along the outside edge, beginning at the outside corner of the platform. At the inside end and resting on the piece erect a 2 by 4 (marked I, figs. 17 and 21) cut to the correct height to fit under the first layer of ceiling. Cut three rafters each 8 feet 7 inches long.

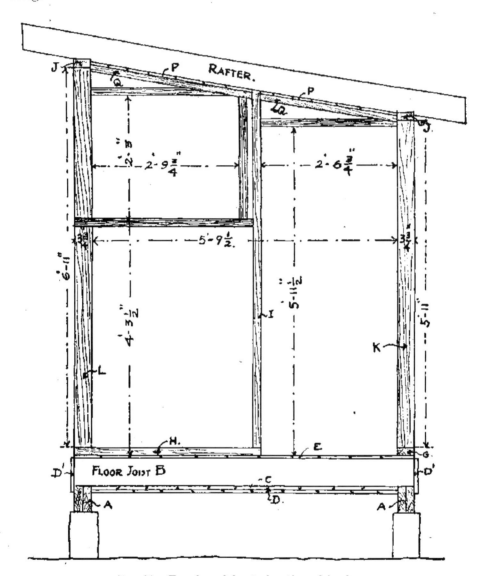

FIG. 21.—Framing of front elevation of ice house.

Nail one of the plates on top of the corner stud K, level it, and support it at the other end by a board placed upright, nail to the platform on the end and at the corner. Place the plate on the stud L, letting it project over the stud 3¾ inches, and support the opposite end by a board erected in the same way as that used to hold up the first plate.

At each end of the building, 3 feet 6 inches from the floor, put in a piece of 2 by 4 (marked M in figs. 18 and 22) set flatwise, and nail to the upright 2 by 4 and to the upright board. Next cut a piece of 2 by 4 6 feet 5 inches long (marked N in figs. 18, 19, and 22) and lay it on the end 2 by 4's (marked M) and nail them together.

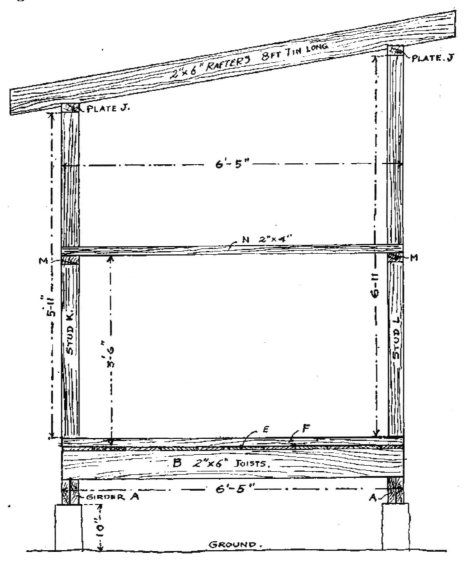

Fig. 22.—Elevation of frame of ice house.

The boards marked O in figures 17 and 18, forming the first layer of the inside lining, should now be put on the ends. The boards are cut just long enough to extend from the floor to the top of the plate. Cut three rafters 2 inches by 6 inches by 8 feet 7 inches and nail to the plates, spaced as shown in figure 18. The frame is now ready to put on the first layer of boards to form the ceiling. The ceiling boards (marked P in figs. 18 and 19) are cut just long enough to reach between the outside faces of the rafters.

A 2 by 4 (marked Q in figs. 19 and 21) is now to be nailed flatwise to the ceiling. The inside edge of the 2 by 4 is set on a line with the 2 by 4's already in place and is for the purpose of forming a support to which the upper ends of the side boards are nailed. After this scantling is nailed in place put on the first inside layer of boards (marked R in figs. 17 and 19). Next put on the first layer of boards forming the outside. The boards for ends of building should be cut to extend from the top of the rafters to the top of the board nailed across the ends of the floor joists (see S, fig. 18). The boards for the side should be cut flush with the top of the rafter and should follow the slope of the roof. The roof is now ready to have the shavings put in place. Use about 100 pounds and then put on the roof boards in two layers with paper between. The roof boards should project over the ends of the rafter about 2 inches and beyond the sides of the building about 1 foot. The roof boards should be covered without delay with whatever kind of covering it is intended to use, as the shavings must not be allowed to get wet or damp.

The roof may be covered with tin, shingles, or one of the prepared roofings, and should be made thoroughly watertight. When putting up the first layer of the boards on the outside of the frame the corner boards can not be put on until the shavings have been packed in the walls. The walls will require about 400 pounds of shavings.

Before the shavings are put in the walls the side of the building containing the doors should be framed as shown in figure 21, then the first layers of boards put on the inside and outside of the wall.

After the shavings are in place put on the corner boards and cover all the walls with a waterproof building paper, lapping the paper at the corners and at the horizontal courses.

The building is now ready to receive the outside layer of boards, which should be put on without delay to prevent as far as possible any moisture getting into the insulation.

The doorways are beveled to receive the doors and to assist in making them fit tightly (see drawing, figs. 17 and 18). After the outside boarding is on, the inside of the room can be papered and sheathed. The paper is put on as follows: Cover the floor with two layers of waterproof paper and turn up on the walls 1 foot all around; then, starting at the floor, lay a course of paper on the walls parallel with the floor. Cut the strip 2 feet longer than the length of the wall and start the paper 1 foot from the corner, then carry around the nearest corner, tack to the wall, and carry around the next corner, doubling the paper at the corners. Put on the next course and lap over the lower course about 4 inches. Put on the remaining courses until the ceiling is reached, when the paper should be turned over and nailed to the ceiling so that the paper covers the corner between the ceiling and the wall. Now lay the ceiling and bring down on the walls about 1 foot. Use care in putting on the paper so that no holes will be punched in it. After the paper is on lay the top floor and ceiling before putting on the side and end walls, using care to make as tight a fit as possible between the floor and walls and the ceiling and walls.

After the walls are finished build the ice crib. The floor of the ice crib is made of 2 by 4 dressed longleaf yellow pine, spaced 2¾ inches apart. The supports for the floor are made by nailing a piece of dressed 2 by 4 inch scantling parallel with the floor to the inside boarding of the house and under each end of the scantling is nailed a 2 by 4 extending from the floor of the house to the underside of the supports. Running across the box nail a piece of 1 by 3 inch flatwise on the ceiling. The strip is so placed that it will be outside of the ice crib and to it are nailed 1 by 3 inch dressed slats spaced about 3 inches apart. The bottom of the slats are nailed to the outside of the first joist of the ice crib. This joist is located 3 feet from the back of the ice crib.

The joist nearest the back of the ice crib is spaced 2¾ inches from the back wall. On the face of this joist between the joist and the wall, nail a strip 1 by 4 inch dressed, letting the strip project 2 inches above the top of the joists. Five inches from the inside end of the ice crib nail a 1 by 4 inch dressed strip across all the joists to form a stop for the ice cakes.

The drip pan under the ice crib is made of a sheet of galvanized corrugated iron. The corrugations run the long way of the room. The sheet is made 2 feet 7 inches wide and 3 feet 4 inches long, the width being the length of the corrugations. A 3-inch galvanized iron gutter 3 feet 4 inches long is riveted to the edge of the sheet on the underside. The sheet should pitch about 2 inches in the width. The high end of the sheet is nailed to the bottom of the first joist and the low end is supported by three straps soldered to the gutter and nailed to the joist above. The gutter should be closed at each end and should pitch about an inch from the front to the back. At the lowest point of the gutter the drain pipe should be attached by soldering. The drain pipe is a piece of gas or water pipe ¾-inch inside diameter and should extend from the gutter through the floor of the house and project below about 12 inches. If a bucket is so placed under the pipe that the bottom of the pipe will be about an inch from the bottom of the bucket, the water from the melting ice will form a water seal that will prevent the outside air from entering the house. At least 2 inches of water should be kept in the bucket to form the seal.

If a drain is provided to carry away the water, the bucket can be omitted, provided a trap is made in the pipe.

The meat should not be stacked on the floor of the building, but racks should be provided. The racks are made by nailing 2 by 4's edgewise against the wall and on the floor. On the face of the 2 by 4's strips 1 by 3 inches spaced about 3 inches apart are securely nailed.

The racks on the floor should not be nailed to the floor, but should be made removable in order to facilitate cleaning.

The racks against the walls are for the purpose of permitting the air to circulate around the meat.

The doors are made of three thicknesses of boards similar to those used in lining the room, nailed to a frame made of dressed 2 by 3's. The frame is first made and covered with a thickness of boards. The box thus formed is filled with shavings and covered with boards. Turn the door over, lay a sheet of paper on the boards, and add another thickness of boards. The edges of the door are to be beveled to fit the door opening. The door must be made smaller than the opening to allow for the canvas and felt that are to be nailed all around the edges of the door and around the door opening. The hinges to hang the door should be extra heavy **T** hinges. The outside of the building should be painted three coats with an oil paint. The efficiency of the house depends upon the tightness with which it is built, and to assist in keeping it tight it is necessary to paint the outside to keep moisture out of the boards, which would cause them to swell and pull away from the inner boards. The paint will also help to keep the boards from the shrinking caused by heat from the sun. The inside of the building should be shellacked or varnished with a waterproof varnish. The varnish will keep the boards from absorbing moisture and causing trouble and will also permit the house to be easily cleaned. The house should be thoroughly cleaned immediately after the meat has been removed.

BILL OF MATERIALS.

FRAME.

2 pieces 2 by 6 inches, 10 feet long, for girders, rough.
2 pieces 2 by 6 inches, 14 feet long, for joists, rough.
3 pieces 2 by 6 inches, 9 feet long, for rafters, rough.
2 cedar posts, 6-inch diameter, 6 feet long.
1 piece 2 by 4 inches, 6 feet long, stud K, dressed.
1 piece 2 by 4 inches, 7 feet long, stud L, dressed.
1 piece 2 by 4 inches, 7 feet long, stud I, dressed.
3 pieces 2 by 4 inches, 10 feet long, for plates and pieces G and M, dressed.
3 pieces 2 by 4 inches, 14 feet long, for pieces F, H, M, Q and framing for doors, dressed.
800 feet b. m. tongued and grooved flooring, dressed.

25 linear feet 1 by 3 inches, for door stop, dressed.
1 piece, 2 by 4 inches, 10 feet long, for beveled jamb of doors, dressed.
2 pieces 2 by 3 inches, 14 feet long, for frame of doors, dressed.

ICE BUNKERS.

1 piece 2 by 4 inches, 6 feet long, for supports, dressed.
7 pieces 2 by 4 inches, 4 feet long, for floor beams, dressed.
1 piece 1 by 4 inches, 8 feet long, for ice stop, dressed.

FLOOR AND WALL RACKS.

3 pieces 2 by 4 inches, 7 feet long, for walls, dressed.
2 pieces 2 by 4 inches, 10 feet long, for floor, dressed.
9 pieces 1 by 3 inches, 14 feet long, slats for ice bunker and wall and floor racks, dressed.

HARDWARE, ETC.

3 extra-heavy T hinges, 18 inches long and screws.
1 pair extra-heavy T hinges, 12 inches long and screws.
1 pair 6-inch handles and screws.
25 pounds 6-penny flooring nails, wire.
5 pounds 10-penny wire nails, common.
5 ounces of 3-ounce tacks.
1 sheet corrugated galvanized iron, 2 feet 6 inches by 4 feet.
1 piece 3-inch galvanized iron gutter, 3 feet 4 inches long, with 3 straps ¾-inch wide by 8 inches long, to fasten gutter to ice floor.
1 piece ¾-inch gas pipe, galvanized, 4 feet 6 inches long.
24 yards canvas or heavy duck, 9 inches wide.
20 yards felt, 6 inches wide, for padding under canvas.
2 gallons waterproof varnish.
2 gallons lead and oil paint.
400 square feet of insulating paper.
70 square feet roofing paper with nails and pitch.
600 pounds dry mill shavings.

PUBLICATIONS OF THE UNITED STATES DEPARTMENT OF AGRICULTURE RELATING TO HOG RAISING.

AVAILABLE FOR FREE DISTRIBUTION BY THE DEPARTMENT.

Meats: Composition and Cooking. (Farmers' Bulletin 34.)

Economical Use of Meat in the Home. (Farmers' Bulletin 391.)

Feeding Hogs in the South. (Farmers' Bulletin 411.)

Hog Houses. (Farmers' Bulletin 438.)

Boys Pig Clubs. (Farmers' Bulletin 566.)

Beef Production in the South. (Farmers' Bulletin 580.)

Breeds of Swine. (Farmers' Bulletin 765.)

Castration of Pigs. (Farmers' Bulletin 780.)

Tuberculosis of Hogs. (Farmers' Bulletin 781.)

Live Stock Classification at County Fairs. (Farmers' Bulletin 822.)

Hog Cholera: Prevention and Treatment. (Farmers' Bulletin 834.)

Utilization of Farm Wastes in Feeding Live Stock. (Farmers' Bulletin 873.)

Swine Management. (Farmers' Bulletin 874.)

Killing Hogs and Curing Pork. (Farmers' Bulletin 913.)

Feeding of Dried Pressed Potatoes to Swine. (Department Bulletin 596.)

Meat Situation in the United States: Part V. Methods and Cost of Marketing Live Stock. (Report 113.)

FOR SALE BY THE SUPERINTENDENT OF DOCUMENTS, GOVERNMENT PRINTING OFFICE, WASHINGTON, D. C.

Feeding Farm Animals. (Farmers' Bulletin 22.) Price, 5 cents.

Meats on the Farm: Butchering, Curing, and Keeping. (Farmers' Bulletin 183.) Price, 5 cents.

Pig Management. (Farmers' Bulletin 205.) Price, 5 cents.

Pasture and Grain Crops for Hogs in the Pacific Northwest. (Farmers' Bulletin 599.) Price, 5 cents.

South American Meat Industry. (Separate 629 from Year Book 1913.) Price, 5 cents.

O